Being an Entrepreneur

The Solopreneur's Guide to Living the Dream Without Losing it!

Ric Thompson

Ric Thompson

Just to say Thank You for Purchasing this Book I want to give you a gift <u>100% absolutely FREE</u>

A Copy of My Special Report

"Outsource Time"

Go to

www.DoneForYouSolutions.com/OutsourceTime
to Receive Your FREE Gift

© 2014

All Rights Reserved. No part of this publication may be reproduced in any form or by any means, including scanning, photocopying, or otherwise without prior written permission of the copyright holder.

Disclaimer and Terms of Use: The Author and Publisher have strived to be as accurate and complete as possible in the creation of this book, notwithstanding the fact that they do not warrant or represent at any time that the contents within are accurate due to the rapidly changing nature of the Internet. While all attempts have been made to verify information provided in this publication, the Author and Publisher assume no responsibility for errors, omissions, or contrary interpretation of the subject matter herein. Any perceived slights of specific persons, peoples, or organizations are unintentional. In practical advice books, like anything else in life, there are no guarantees of income made or health benefits received. This book is not intended for use as a source of medical, legal, business, accounting or financial advice. All readers are advised to seek services of competent professionals in medical, legal, business, accounting, and finance matters.

Printed in the United States of America

Table of Contents

INTRODUCTION	7
BEING AN ENTREPRENEUR	8
How Entrepreneurs Affect the World Around Them	9
The Strengths and Characteristics of an Entrepreneur	11
Back to You and Your Business	13
WHAT'S YOUR ENTREPRENEURIAL SCORE?	15
LESSON 1: TIME MANAGEMENT AND EFFECTIVENESS	17
The Real Value of Your Time	17
Time Evaluation Exercise	18
The Key to Effective Time Management	21
What Happens When Entrepreneurs Don't Effectively Manage their Time?	23
Work Suffers	*23*
Personal Life Suffers	*24*
Health Suffers	*24*
How Effectively Do You Manage Your Time Right Now?	25
Time Management Skills that Work	26
Goal Setting	*26*
Tasking	*26*
Priorities	*27*
Evaluating Where Your Time Management Skills Excel	27
The 80/20 Principle	28
What Keeps Entrepreneurs from Being More Productive?	29
Perfectionism	*29*
Procrastination	*30*
Never Saying No	*30*
Not Delegating	*30*

WHERE YOUR TIME MANAGEMENT SKILLS NEED IMPROVEMENT	31
TIME MANAGEMENT TOOLS	33
Online Time Management Tools	*34*
Offline Time Management Tools	*35*
WHAT TIME MANAGEMENT TOOL IS RIGHT FOR YOU?	36

LESSON 2: PERSONAL DEVELOPMENT – STRENGTHS, KNOWING YOURSELF, AND PERPETUAL GROWTH   38

WHY IT IS IMPORTANT TO KNOW YOURSELF TO BE SUCCESSFUL IN BUSINESS	39
WHAT ARE YOUR STRENGTHS WEAKNESSES OPPORTUNITIES AND THREATS?	41
Strengths	*42*
Weaknesses	*43*
Opportunities	*43*
Threats	*43*
PERSONAL AND PROFESSIONAL DEVELOPMENT TOOLS	45
Mastermind Groups	*45*
Seminars, Online Courses, and Workshops	*46*
Learning Style Inventory	*46*
PLANNING FOR THE FUTURE: CONTINUOUS DEVELOPMENT AND ASSESSMENT	47
Why it is Important to Plan for the Future	*48*
What You Have to Gain	*48*
How Much Time Do You Spend on Yourself?	*49*

LESSON 3: HAVING A LIFE OUTSIDE OF THE BUSINESS   50

EVALUATING YOUR PRIORITIES	50
IS YOUR LIFE IN BALANCE?	52
Without Balance We Neglect the Things that are Really Important to Us	*54*
THE BENEFITS OF LIVING A BALANCED LIFE	55
Happiness	*57*
A Sense of Peace and Calm	*57*
Better Run Business	*57*

Is Your Life in Balance?	58
Tools to Bring Balance to Your Life	59
How are You Going to Add More Fun to Your Life?	63

INSPIRED ACTION — 66

WHAT'S YOUR ENTREPRENEURIAL SCORE NOW? — 67

CONCLUSION — 70

Introduction

I want to thank you and congratulate you for downloading *"Being an Entrepreneur, The Solopreneur's Guide to Living the Dream Without Losing it!"*.

This guide provides very solid basics for you to better understand what it means to be an entrepreneur and what you need to succeed in your own business. It is meant to be a fun exploration into the possibilities of how you can take these concepts and fully embrace the life of an entrepreneur. You'll change your life and your world for the better, becoming a happier and more productive YOU, both personally and professionally.

Once you complete this guide, you will have a roadmap for a balanced life both inside and outside your business.

After reading this guide, you will understand why time management is so important to entrepreneurs and how to live a balanced life while also building a successful business.

If you are ready to take your business to the next level and blow past the competition, this guide provides a starting place to assess your strengths, manage your time, and ensure balance in your life. You know the saying: all work and no play makes Jack, or Jill, a dull person. Life is neither all business nor all fun, but an appropriate amount of both.

With the help of "***Being an Entrepreneur,***" you're on your way to achieving just about anything you can imagine. Thanks again for downloading, I hope you enjoy it!

Ric Thompson

Being an Entrepreneur

"The critical ingredient is getting off your butt and doing something. It's as simple as that. A lot of people have ideas, but there are few who decide to do something about them now. Not tomorrow. Not next week. But today. The true entrepreneur is a doer, not a dreamer."
- - Nolan Bushnell, founder of Atari and Chuck E. Cheese's

I love this quote because it doesn't pull any punches. True, an entrepreneur, as you well know, has to have a dream, a vision. However, that vision doesn't become reality without focused effort and ACTION.

You know this too.

In fact, if you've been in business for more than five minutes, there may be times when you wonder if you'll ever get everything done. Being an entrepreneur can be HARD work, but the rewards and the freedom are AMAZING.

Now before we get too far ahead of ourselves, it is important to recognize what you've accomplished...

Congratulations for being one of those people who got off their butt and did something. You're an entrepreneur! You own, or are in the process of creating, your own company.

As a business owner, you've likely noticed a few changes in your life – and that's probably an understatement. Your life may feel like it's in total chaos. Your priorities have probably changed. Housework and socialization may have fallen to the bottom of your "to do" list.

You're now responsible to customers, contractors or employees, and you're responsible for your own income. Your friends and family are still there and want to spend time with you, and you have your own personal interests and hobbies. Surely those haven't left your radar. You've probably realized that there are too many things to do and too little time to do them all.

Welcome to the world of business ownership!

But seriously, part of being an entrepreneur is learning about balance. It doesn't happen at once. However, with the right knowledge and approach, you will be able to find that balance. There are a few tricks of the trade. Some of these tricks or strategies will work better for you than others.

Before we get into some of these life-balancing strategies, let's first take a look at your value as an entrepreneur.

How Entrepreneurs Affect the World Around Them

While it may seem like every person you meet has the dream of opening their own business, for the majority of them, it is just a dream. It's too bad, really. As a culture and a race, we've received so much benefit from those who have decided to make their dreams a reality. Consider Jeff Bezos, who has quite possibly been the biggest influence on online shopping today.

How many people shop online? E-commerce transactions in 2007 reached $228 billion and are expected to reach $258 billion in 2008. That's a lot of online shopping that might not have existed at this level if it hadn't been for Amazon.com.

Amazon.com and the concept that shopping online – whether it is books, clothing, or a new car, is part of the new collective consciousness. Jeff Bezos, and his dream to bring the ability to shop from the comfort of your couch, has changed lives. Today Amazon's mission statement is:

> **"Our vision is to be earth's most customer centric company; to build a place where people can come to find and discover anything they might want to buy online."**

Thanks Jeff!

But let's step much farther back in time and take a look at something you most likely take for granted – your car. Not only did Henry Ford really change our day-to-day lives, the mass production of the automobile changed everything. Without it, travel industry wouldn't really exist in its current form. Can you imagine a world without automotive transportation? Entrepreneurs, past, present, and future, have a significant influence on the world.

What impact will YOU have?

Perhaps you've heard of the butterfly theory, or chaos theory. It is how one singular event like a butterfly flapping its wings in Costa Rica can influence changes all around the world. Maybe the butterfly flaps its wings and the tiny air currents create changes in the atmosphere that ultimately cause a tornado. This tornado destroys a farm which provides beef to half of the meat packing plants in the country. Beef prices go up and the high prices stimulate a new trend of eating vegetarian. No one would initially connect a vegetarian trend with a butterfly, but there it is. It happened. Likewise your actions can have a similar effect on the world. Your business will have an influence on the lives of others all around the world. It is frightening and exhilarating at the same time. Such responsibility!

Perhaps you're sitting at your desk reading this and thinking, "I don't want that responsibility, I just want to own my own business." Ask yourself why you want to run your own business. Somewhere in your list of answers you'll find you're ready and excited about your ability to change peoples' lives. It's something all entrepreneurs have in common.

The Strengths and Characteristics of an Entrepreneur

So what characteristics and strengths do you have in common with entrepreneurs all around the world – past, present, and future? People like Henry Ford and Jeff Bezos?

Entrepreneurs have faith in their dreams, are not afraid of hard work, and know the value of being in control of their own destiny. Owning a business isn't easy and it takes great creativity and perseverance. Entrepreneurs, like yourself, have priorities and strive for balance. No one is perfect; however, the entrepreneur knows life is about balance. It's about working hard and playing hard. We'll talk a lot about that in Lesson 3 of this guide. What else do entrepreneurs have in common? They possess the knowledge and ability to take advantage of the resources around them for the better of the world, despite challenges and obstacles. Successful entrepreneurs understand that it is important to focus on their strengths.

Here's a great example of how perseverance, focusing on strengths and taking advantage of opportunities and resources can help an entrepreneur change the world…

On top of busy careers in public and motivational speaking, Jack Canfield and Mark Victor Hansen listened to their supporters and decided to put together a book of stories. Translating those shared stories onto the written page was a challenge neither of them expected. Finding time in their busy schedules to record these stories on paper was difficult, and editing them went above and beyond the time they had in their schedule. It took them three years to put together a small sampling of sixty-eight stories. They believed it would require 101 stores to make a successful book. What did they do? They did something we're going to talk about later in this lesson: they asked for help. I'm sure they already had people transcribing and editing their stories. However, that wasn't enough. These two men already had full lives and a thriving business.

Jack and Mark, to fill their requirement of 101 stories, asked other professional speakers to submit their favorite stories for publication. Guess what happened? Tons of amazing stories landed on their desk. They not only had enough for one book, they had enough for several books. The problems didn't stop there. They now faced an uphill struggle to publish the book. No one wanted it. They were rejected by 140 different publishers. No one thought it would work. But when an entrepreneur has a dream and is willing to work hard to make it a reality, willing to work hard to better the lives of others, they don't take no for an answer. In 1992, Jack and Mark attended the American Booksellers' Association Convention. At the convention, they spent days talking to editors and sharing their vision of how their book would uplift humanity by helping people open their hearts, rekindle their spirits and give them the courage to pursue their dreams. One of the lucky editors was a man by the name of Peter Vegso, President of Health Communications Inc. He understood what they were trying to accomplish, and the rest is history.

Since then they've added 169 more titles in 41 languages, selling a combined total of more that 112 million books! Hundreds of millions of people have been positively influenced by the Chicken Soup for the Soul book series. Jack Canfield and Mark Victor Hansen stuck to their beliefs: they worked hard, they utilized resources around them and they accomplished their goal.

Back to You and Your Business

Your business affects lives, yours and everyone you do business with, in ways you can't even begin to imagine. You helping one single person, no matter what your business, will potentially affect thousands if not millions. Considering the implications can be both uplifting and overwhelming. In fact, simply being an entrepreneur can be overwhelming. It can, quite frankly, take over your life.

How many times have you missed going out with friends or doing something that you were looking forward to because you had too much work to do? How many times have you snapped at someone because you feel overwhelmed and stressed out?

You're not alone. I'd venture that each and every entrepreneur, including Jeff Bezos and Henry Ford, had moments where they thought they were going to implode. Moments where they snapped. Moments where they maybe even cried or threw things. Being an entrepreneur isn't easy. If it were, everyone would be doing it.

Being an entrepreneur and having the responsibility of affecting the lives of others can be a good thing, and it can be a very destructive thing. We want to keep it from being destructive!

This is a pitfall we don't want you to fall into because balance, organization, and self-growth are important parts of being an entrepreneur. As important as being able to sell, manage employees, and grow your business.

What's Your Entrepreneurial Score?

Before we get started, spend a few minutes and take this evaluation based on how "Entrepreneurial" you are today. You'll retake it again at the end of the guide to see where you've made progress. It's a great tool to evaluate what you've learned.

Grab a notebook to use for capturing your responses, reactions, thoughts, and actions as you read through this guide and complete the exercises.

On a scale of 1-10 (10 being the highest), rank where you currently stand in life and in business. Once you've completed this guide you'll be taking this evaluation again to see where you've improved.

I know the exact dollar value of my time.

1   2   3   4   5   6   7   8   9   10

I know what my strengths are and have systems in place to help my focus on them.

1   2   3   4   5   6   7   8   9   10

I know what my weaknesses are and have plans for how to get other people to handle them for me.

1   2   3   4   5   6   7   8   9   10

I have systems in place to effectively and efficiently manage my time

1   2   3   4   5   6   7   8   9   10

I know what my time priorities are and have a plan for how to make sure my business doesn't take over my entire life

1   2   3   4   5   6   7   8   9   10

I am confident that I can drive my business, not have my business drive me.

1   2   3   4   5   6   7   8   9   10

SCORING

Add up all the numbers you circled. _____

Divide the total number by 6

Record your "Entrepreneurial Score" here _____

Lesson 1: Time Management and Effectiveness

"An entrepreneur tends to bite off a little more than he can chew hoping he'll quickly learn how to chew it."
- Roy Ash, co-founder of Litton Industries

The Real Value of Your Time

Read the quote at the top of the page. Does this describe you? It describes the majority of entrepreneurs out there. So tell me, how quickly are you learning to chew what you've bitten off?

There are only 24 hours in every day, 168 hours in a week, and 365 days in a year. As an entrepreneur you've probably realized this more than you ever wanted to. You likely have tons to do, and the tasks never seem to end. Everyone has the same amount of time. It's what you DO with that time that makes the difference.

Before we can talk about how to manage your time in the most effective way possible, it is first important to understand the value of your time. It's easy enough to look at an old paycheck stub and acknowledge that your time was valued at a certain amount after taxes. However, when you're an entrepreneur, you don't have those paycheck stubs. You're responsible for your own paycheck. You're also responsible for your working hours and what you do during that time.

Before you can determine how best to spend your time, take this exercise to evaluate the value of your time.

Time Evaluation Exercise

The purpose of this exercise is to help you evaluate the value of your time (From Dan Kennedy's No B.S. Time Management for Entrepreneurs). Use a page in your notebook to capture your responses to the steps below.

Step 1 List your minimum earnings target for the year
$_____

Step 2 Divide by # of work hours in the year
/_____ =

Step 3 Minimum hourly rate
$_____

For example, if you work full time in your business and take three weeks off a year, the hours would look like this: 52 weeks a year - 3 weeks' vacation = 49 weeks

49 weeks multiplied by 5 days a week = 245 days. This is the number of days you work in a year given that you take three weeks' vacation.

245 annual work days multiplied by 8 hours a day =1960 work hours per year. If you work fewer hours a day then that number will change. Likewise if you don't take three weeks' vacation (hopefully you take more), then your annual work days will be different. This is a sample to demonstrate how the calculation works.

Continuing with the sample numbers, a sample calculation for someone working full time in their business with a minimum earnings target of $50,000 would be

Minimum earnings target of $50,000 divided by 1960 annual hours worked = $25.51/hour

However, there's a hitch in the calculation. Do you really think that for all the work you do during the day, you're making your hourly value? Not likely. Answering emails isn't necessarily a profit-building task. And what about when you spend 30 minutes on the phone with a contractor? That time may not be contributing to your hourly value.

When you're working, you're not really making your minimum earnings target every hour. NO ONE is that effective, and you DO have to do non-revenue producing activities sometimes. So look at your average workweek and estimate how much of your time is actually PRODUCTIVE. It's less than you think.

A ten-year study, published in the Harvard Business Review, showed that 90% of the time spent by employees and managers is unproductive "busy work".

That means their average productive time was only 10%!

One study of Fortune 500 CEOs showed they averaged only 28 MINUTES of productive time a day. Holy smokes! Having only 28 minutes of productive time each day isn't accomplishing much. Surely you're more productive than that.

Or are you?

In a couple of pages, you'll find an exercise designed to help you see how productive your time really is. This exercise is always an eye-opener, even for the most productive people. You might be surprised what tasks consume the majority of your time.

However, for argument's sake let's say you're TWICE as productive as the average employee or manager – you're productive 20% of the time.

Here's your NEW calculation

Step 1 List your minimum earnings target for the year
$_____

Step 2 Multiply your annual working hours by your time productivity multiple   _____ * X% =

Step 3 Divide your minimum earnings by your total in Step 2 Minimum hourly rate

_____ / _____ =

Step 4 New Minimum Hourly Rate $_____

Your new calculation might look something like this:

Minimum earnings target $50,000 divided by (1960 annual working hrs multiplied by 20%) = $127.55/hr.

That's a better looking number, isn't it? What does this new number tell you? If you can increase your productivity each day, your hourly value goes up tremendously. So too do your chances of meeting or exceeding your target revenue. It also stresses the importance of focusing on strengths and profitable tasks, of prioritizing your time, managing your time, and of finding other ways to get the non-productive time-stealing tasks taken care of.

Let's look at how to better manage your time so that you can reach your target revenue and make each day more productive, more enjoyable, and more profitable.

"If you want to make good use of your time, you've got to know what's most important and then give it all you've got."
-Lee Iacocca

The Key to Effective Time Management

Being effective is about getting the most important things done. The late Gary Halbert, arguably one of the greatest copywriters in the world, created the family crest industry as we know it through direct mail. At one point he had legions of secretaries working for him doing little except preparing bank deposits every day. He would often go into the office, lock the door, and ignore the crises happening outside.

Outside the door, all heck might be breaking loose. People would be banging on the door saying there was a problem with the printer, there could be a crisis with the mail delivery, one of the trucks used to take deposits to the bank could be broken. It didn't matter. Gary would ignore them all. He'd lock the door and write marketing copy.

Why? He had staff who could handle the problems, even though they often didn't want to or think they could, and he knew what it was important for him to do. His strength was writing marketing copy. It was what he'd built his business and his fortune around. It was what paid the salaries of the people on the other side of the door. He knew his strengths, and he hired others to handle everything else.

What are your strengths? Where is your time most productive, focused, and profitable?

For example, take a look at your own life. Many entrepreneurs, especially those who work from home, have household chores that can be distracting from more productive tasks.

You know how much your time is worth and how much you WANT it to be worth by using the calculations presented earlier.

Consider hiring a housekeeper as your first outsourced employee or contractor. Seriously.

Say right now your time is worth $50/hour. Does it make any sense at all to scrub your own toilets or do your own laundry when you can hire someone to do that for $10/hour?

Additionally, is it worth your time to do your books and invoices when you can hire someone to do them for $15/hour and they take half the time it would take you to do the same thing? If your time ISN'T worth what you want it to be yet, are you really going to be able to increase that value while you're wasting time on tasks that someone else should be doing?

It's about the value of your time now and your desired value of your time. If you're trying to boost your hourly rate to even the very modest number in the example above, $127.55, you absolutely CAN NOT be wasting time on lesser valued tasks. If that means letting the laundry pile up for a while, just make sure the piles aren't a fire hazard. If you can't eat off the floor because it hasn't been scrubbed in a month, then don't eat off the floor.

Focusing your time on the tasks that generate a direct profit and increasing your hourly value is imperative for successful entrepreneurs. Your time is too valuable to be spent scrubbing toilets or doing the bookkeeping.

This is such an important concept, in our book "***Lead: Strategic Management and Leadership for Innovators and Solopreneurs,***" [http://www.amazon.com/dp/B00NRVWE3A] we have a full lesson devoted to hiring and outsourcing.

Being an entrepreneur means making choices, setting priorities, and sticking with them.

When you truly know what your time needs to be worth, it's MUCH easier to make intelligent decisions.

What Happens When Entrepreneurs Don't Effectively Manage their Time?

Being aware of your hourly value is only the beginning. To be successful, it is important to be able to manage your time effectively. Time management means not allowing distractions. It means handling the important tasks first, the tasks that increase your hourly value. There are definite ramifications to poor time management.

Work Suffers

Lack of effective time management means hours and hours spent on tasks that are not important, leaving only a little bit of time for the projects that really do affect your bottom line. For example, how often have you spent an entire morning on email, only to find at the end of the day that many major tasks weren't accomplished, and you either had to rush through them and produce less than ideal results, or the tasks get put off, resulting in a loss of income or potential income?

Lack of effective time management also means trying to handle too many tasks at once. Multitasking may seem like a good idea, but tasks are accomplished much faster when they're dealt with one at a time. Juggle too much at once, and a ball is bound to drop from time to time. Unfortunately the ball you drop may be the most important one.

Personal Life Suffers

What do you do if something doesn't get accomplished during normal work hours? Do you work on it in the evenings or on weekends when you could be spending time with your friends and family?

Health Suffers

Working 80 hours a week isn't good for anyone. Sleep, laughter, fun, and a personal life are all important to your mental health, and guess what – they're important to your physical health too.

According to the American Medical Association, when faced with chronic stress and an over-activated autonomic nervous system, people begin to see physical symptoms. The first symptoms are relatively mild, like chronic headaches and a decreased immune system. As stress continues and increases more serious health problems can develop including:

- Depression
- Diabetes
- Hair loss
- Heart disease
- Hyperthyroidism
- Obesity
- Obsessive-compulsive or anxiety disorder

- Sexual dysfunction
- Tooth and gum disease
- Ulcers

In fact, the American Medical Association also estimates that as many as 90% of doctor's visits are for symptoms that are at least partially stress-related!

How Effectively Do You Manage Your Time Right Now?

Track your time over the next week. Don't modify your behavior. Actually and honestly track how much time you spend on each task. If it takes four hours each day to answer email, then track that time. If you spend two hours brainstorming marketing headlines, copy, keywords, or even ideas, then track that time. This is important. When you know where your time is focused, and you know what tasks produce a profit (and increase your hourly value), then you have information to base decisions and actions on.

This exercise will help you understand how you are spending your time right now. Once you have a handle on how effective your current time management skills are, it's time to take a look at what's working for you, what isn't working for you and how to modify your habits to become more productive, more profitable, and to make time in your life for the fun stuff!

> *Dost thou love life, then do not squander time,*
> *for that's the stuff life is made of.*
> -Benjamin Franklin

Time Management Skills that Work

Some of the tricks or strategies to stay on track are simple in theory, yet it takes focus to put them into practice. Let's examine three strategies that work to keep your days, weeks, and months under control and productive.

Goal Setting

Strategize goals for your day, week, and month. Of course goal setting CAN be taken too far and can often be used to set completely unrealistic goals for yourself that demoralize you. That isn't productive or effective.

Instead of using unachievable, lofty goals, here it is better to set what we'll call "targets." A baseline target which is the minimum required for success, a growth or stretch target which provides a doable challenge, and an out-of-the-park target which is still within the realm of possibility and which you'd be ecstatic if you hit. That way you don't have to hit a "bull's-eye" every time to achieve success, and you can use the ring that you're hitting (the baseline, growth, or out-of-the-park target) as a training tool to do better next time.

Success is a process, not a destination. Also, targets make it easier for us to focus on one task at a time. There are dangers in multi-tasking, including losing focus on the important tasks of your day, week, or month. When you set targets for your day, you're better able to focus on getting the job done.

Tasking

Having all of your tasks in one central location is not only a super way to keep track of what needs to be done; it also shows you what has been accomplished. There's nothing much worse than spending a day being busy without having any results to show at the end of the day. Tasks are defined as small work projects. It is sometimes helpful to break larger projects into smaller tasks.

Priorities

Ha! You thought you were finished when you listed everything you needed to do for the day, week, and month, didn't you? Well, if you take a look at your list on any given day, some items or tasks are more important than others, right? For example, updating your website with your new content may be more important than emailing your VA to check in. So not only are tasks important, ranking them by importance will make each day much more productive and will make you more efficient. I want to take it one step further and recommend tackling your more challenging tasks during your most productive times.

For example, if you're a morning person, don't handle administrative tasks then, handle the tasks that focus on your strengths and the tasks that have the most profitable results. In other words, handle the tasks that raise your hourly value by increasing your profits.

Evaluating Where Your Time Management Skills Excel

To better understand what is working for you right now, let's take a look at the areas where you feel you're strong; where your time management skills are already working quite well. Once you know where you're strong, it will be easier to let go of or find alternatives to the areas where you struggle. Use your notebook to record your responses to the following questions and prompts.

What are your strengths?

When you're looking at the tasks you handle each and every day, what tasks are you efficient with?

What tasks are easy to focus on?

What tasks absorb your heart, attention, and passion?

What areas of time management are working for you?

Where do you feel like you're getting it right?

Fill in the blank: I am proud of my ability to_____

Now you have a good grasp on where your strengths lie, right? Let's take a look at a phenomenon called the 80/20 principle. This theory will help you focus the strengths you just documented in the worksheet and make them work for you both in your personal and in your business life.

The 80/20 Principle

The 80/20 principle means that 80% of your outcomes come from 20% of your inputs. In other words, for many phenomena, 80% of consequences stem from 20% of the causes, or 80% of the profits of your business will result from 20% of your effort.

You can also apply this principle to your personal life and consider that 80% of your happiness stems from 20% of your relationships.

In business, the principle can be applied to demonstrate that 20% of the customers contribute 80% of the profits.

So, what can you take from this principle?

The message is simple enough – focus on the activities and tasks which produce the best outcomes for you.

In business, focus on your strengths and the tasks which produce a higher hourly value.

Personally, focus on the hobbies, friends, beliefs, and family members that bring you the most joy and satisfaction.

What Keeps Entrepreneurs from Being More Productive?

We all have hurdles to overcome and hang-ups, to be sure. Some of these hurdles and hang-ups keep us from attaining what we desire. Including:

Perfectionism

This is often a crutch for those who don't know what else to do, wasting time and keeping you from moving forward. For those who are slapdash slobs, too little perfectionism can kill the business. Pick the TRULY important areas and be diligent about them. Perfectionism is the plague of many, and a lack of perfectionism is the plague of the rest. Finding a balance is the key. Do your best, work your hardest on the tasks you choose to do, and when you've done your best, let it go. Nothing is completely perfect.

Procrastination

While this can be an effective tool if used to procrastinate on the stupid time wasters, it can be the kiss of death if you procrastinate on the important parts of your business. Reflect on what you procrastinate on – why do you procrastinate on these particular tasks? For some, it is the desire to be perfect or a fear of failure. For others, it is the dread of handling the mundane tasks. Once you're able to evaluate why you procrastinate, you can make better decisions about what to do with the tasks you procrastinate on.

Never Saying No

> *"The art of leadership is saying no, not saying yes. It is very easy to say yes."*
> *- Tony Blair.*

Saying yes to everything means not having any time to focus on profitable and productive tasks. Learning to say no is an absolute MUST for any entrepreneur. If you're someone that has trouble saying no, overcome it. Begin by telling people you need to think about it if the word "no" won't form on your lips. "I need to think about it," will ease the transition to "No, I'm not interested" or "No, I can't do that." Seriously, learning to say no will change your life.

Not Delegating

Having done some of the exercises and worksheets prior to this, you've realized how valuable your time is and how important it is to focus on productive tasks. Delegating is one of the absolute best ways to free your time so that you can be more productive. You can't and definitely

SHOULDN'T be trying to do it all – delegate, delegate, delegate. (That DOES NOT mean abdicate, abdicate, abdicate! You are still ultimately responsible for everything that goes on, so make sure you and or your team can handle what you take on. We talk more about how to do this in *"Lead: Strategic Management and Leadership for Innovators and Solopreneurs".*)
[http://www.amazon.com/dp/B00NRVWE3A]

Where Your Time Management Skills Need Improvement

This exercise will help you identify what isn't working for you right now. Where are your time management and productivity skills lacking? How often do you find yourself saying, "There just aren't enough hours in the day?" We've all felt that. However, barring your ability to change time – what can you do to fill in the gaps?

Earlier we talked about how entrepreneurs like Jack Canfield and Mark Victor Hansen, the Chicken Soup for the Soul guys, called on experts, speakers, and other people they knew in the industry to send them stories for their book. They understood that they had a gap to fill in the desire to see their book come to fruition.

Another solution might be to take advantage of resources. Task your family with taking over some of the household chores if that is a possibility. Hire or outsource help on the tasks you don't enjoy, lack skill in, or simply take up too much of your time. We talk in depth about outsourcing in *"Lead: Strategic Management and Leadership for Innovators and Solopreneurs,"* where we cover finding, hiring, and managing people.

Answer the following questions in your notebook to help you determine what tasks and time management skills need to be reviewed, and possibly how you can better manage your time. Answer these questions honesty and openly – you're the only one reading this!

What time management skills could you improve on?

Do you procrastinate?

Are you a perfectionist?

Are you unable to say no?

Do you delegate?

Why do you feel you have these habits or behaviors?

Where can you improve your time management?

Fill in the blank: I need help with _____

What are some ideas on how you can get the help/assistance you need?

Now you know where your time management skills are strong and where they need work. You know what your strengths are and how important it is to focus on your strengths and increasing your productive time. You know that productive hours and better time management lead toward more profits and that unproductive time can be managed and improved with several different tools and strategies. Keeping your current time management skills and weaknesses in mind, let's take a look at what time management tools can do for you.

> *"Drive thy business, let not that drive thee."*
> -Benjamin Franklin

Time Management Tools

Walk into any Franklin Covey Store, and one can quickly become a Franklin Covey devotee. It's easy to spend hundreds of dollars on time management paraphernalia, get home, spend hours setting it up, and committing to the system, only to find out a week or a month later that it isn't really working for you. This isn't your fault, it isn't your weakness. It is just not the right system for you.

Before we get started talking about time management tools, it is important to understand that time management needs to be driven by priorities. Too much time management stuff out there forgets to take the big picture into consideration. You'll see tons of books and computer programs that will help you arrange your life so you can be neatly organized and "get it all done".

The question they don't generally address is "DO YOU REALLY NEED TO GET THAT DONE?" Does it really matter if your desk is clean at the end of each day? Does the filing REALLY have to be done every week, especially if you're the one doing it?

Being an entrepreneur means you have to keep the big picture in mind even when you're working in the trenches on the details. Prioritize YOUR time and find a way to have other people fill in the gaps.

You may have your time scheduled to the nth degree, but when push comes to shove, if there's no revenue coming in, does it REALLY matter if you miss that networking meeting where you never get a lead anyway, when you could be working on learning more effective lead generation tactics? Does is really matter if your monthly financials are a week late being done if you're behind on the latest project for your biggest client?

And who cares if the paper clips are color coded and organized by size, or if every comma and semicolon on your website is absolutely perfect? You'd be surprised how many "perfectionists" are paralyzed by these things. The question and the yard stick is: Are you getting the important parts of your business handled?

Whether a Franklin Planner helps you accomplish and prioritize your tasks, or a dog-eared notebook with a chewed up pencil gets the job done, the important thing is to get the job done. That being said, here are a few "time management" resources to help you find your way.

Online Time Management Tools

Sometimes the best tools are the simplest. Online you'll find an abundance of time management tools, including tools which will email you your tasks, brainstorms, grocery lists, and the like. Google and Outlook offer tasking and calendar tools which are fairly straightforward. The benefit of online tools is that if you work from your computer the majority of your day, the online tools are right there at your fingertips. If you're working with a team of contractors, then project management tools can be helpful because they'll keep you apprised of what your contractors are accomplishing, freeing you up to focus on your tasks.

Here are a few of the thousands of options available to you:

- Google email and Google Calendar offers email and calendars, and the home page has task list widgets you can install. You need a Google account to access these features, but they're free with an account. www.google.com

- Microsoft Outlook. This is a calendar, email, contact management, and tasking tool. It is very easy to use and comes installed on many computers. http://office.microsoft.com/en-us/outlook/default.aspx

- Hive Minder is a task management, content management, and project management system. You can use it to organize both yourself and your contractors or employees. There are various levels of membership from free to professional. http://hiveminder.com/splash/

- Tada List is a to-do list that goes with you from your computer to your phone. http://www.tadalist.com/

- Backpack is a task management, to-do list, online program. It includes a calendar and the ability to share lists. http://www.backpackit.com/

Offline Time Management Tools

Offline the good old pocket planner has a long-standing history of success. The good thing about pocket planners, electronic or paper, is that you can carry them with you, and whenever you're reminded of a task, you can quickly add it to your list or check your calendar. The bad thing…it's always with you, and it takes strength of mind to "forget" about work for a while. We'll talk about finding a balance between life and business in Lesson 3.

Franklin Covey and DayTimer are two popular brands. However, like online tools, it is important to find a system that works for you.

What Time Management Tool is Right for You?

It is entirely possible that you're already using one or two or ten different time management tools. This exercise will help you figure out which ones are working for you. It's easy to become stuck in the routine of using these tools. However, if they're not making your time more productive and more profitable, what good are they?

Take a look at the tools you're using. Analyze why they are working, what parts are working, and what isn't working to help you move forward toward a time management plan that really works for you. This helps you maximize and prioritize your time wisely, resulting in more profits and more free time. Record your responses to the questions and prompts below in your notebook.

What time management tools are you currently using?

Are these tools working for you?

If only part of the tool is working for you (e.g. the task list does a great job at reminding you what needs to be done, but you're not using it to prioritize tasks), then write that down too.

Why are the tools working for you, and why not?

What tools will you look into?

Why?

What must your time management tools have to help you stay on track and be productive?

> *When you know your own strengths and weaknesses, you are better able to know those of others. Once you do, managing people becomes an optimization game, where everyone wins.*
> *-Floyd Maxwell*

Lesson 2: Personal Development – Strengths, Knowing Yourself, and Perpetual Growth

How well do you know yourself? What are your strengths? What are your weaknesses? What have you done to commit to your continued growth and development? These are all important questions to ask yourself. They're pivotal to your success, happiness, and satisfaction.

The larger part of being an entrepreneur is being wise about your strengths and limitations, and what to do with them. No one is all things encompassed in one great package. When you know what your strengths are, and conversely when you know your limitations too, it gives you the power, courage, and information to make wise decisions about your business.

For example, imagine running a business where your number one way to make sales and contacts is public speaking. In theory, public speaking, meeting new people, and sharing inspirational stories may sound like fun.

However, if you're terminally shy or just uncomfortable in front of people, then this isn't the right task for you. That doesn't mean your business won't work, it just means attacking the problems from a different angle. Maybe you hire a dynamic public speaker, maybe you stick to video presentations where you don't have to be in front of huge groups of people, or maybe you find an alternative method of selling your product or service. Knowing your strengths, and weaknesses, gives you power.

That said, personal development is the key to your future as an entrepreneur. It starts with knowing yourself, constantly learning and improving, then adapting yourself and your business.

There are a few truths in life. One is that change is constant. I don't imagine Henry Ford could picture the world we live in today. I don't suspect he ever dreamed of the average American owning 2.5 cars, or of a world where cars would go at 300 mph, or that they could run on electricity, or that gasoline would cost more than $3.00 per gallon. But I bet if Henry Ford were alive today, he'd figure out a way to not only adapt to the new environment but to capitalize on it, and we'd all be the better for it.

Continually educating yourself, not only in areas where you're strong in business and where you have definite skill, but in areas you'd like to explore, is one of the best ways to continue to stay on top of your game as an entrepreneur. It will keep your mind fresh and open to new ideas and opportunities. Plus, it'll just make you a better person.

Why It Is Important to Know Yourself to be Successful in Business

Imagine trying to run a business and handle everything yourself. Maybe that isn't a stretch of the imagination, maybe that's exactly where you are right now. When you know yourself, your strengths and weaknesses, it offers many benefits that a business just cannot be successful without.

It enables you to focus on your strengths. When you know what you're truly good at, you know where to focus your time and energy. If you're excellent at writing copy then that is what you should be doing. Why? Passion and skill will bring reward, both financial and personal. If you spend your days working on tasks you're unskilled in, then not only are you not being as productive as you could be, you're not enjoying what you're doing, and you're not focusing your time on profitable, pleasing, and productive endeavors.

For example, think of something you're good at. Got it in your head? Now think about the last time you performed that skill. Think about how you felt when you were doing the task. Did the time go by quickly? Were you productive and efficient? Did you produce good results?

Now think about the last time you performed a task you weren't good at. What was this experience like? Did you find it difficult to focus? Did the time drag? Did you find ten other things that needed to be accomplished while you were doing this one task? Seriously, I bet the laundry started to look more interesting than doing this task, right?

When you're able to focus on your strengths, the rewards are significant. Your results are professional, you feel proud, and this results in both profits and pleasure. That's what being in business is about.

It gives you the power to understand and compensate for the weaknesses. So what do you do with the tasks you're not so skilled at? Well, when you understand your weaknesses, your options are much wider. What you do about those tasks you're not so skilled with is up to you. You could hire an expert to handle the task. You could ask for help and advice. You could even schedule a day to handle all of these tasks. How you deal with it is up to you. The point is that recognizing your weaknesses gives you the power to make appropriate decisions.

If you're awful at programming and coding, then why sit for hours at your computer trying to figure it out? You're punishing yourself, the product isn't going to be what you want, and someone else could handle the job in a tenth of the time and probably for much less than what it's costing you in time, money, and sanity.

Focusing on your strengths helps you grow as a person and an entrepreneur. If you're not growing, you're dying, and the same is true for your business. When you know your strengths, you can focus on those, improve those. Your strengths are what will make you successful.

For example, endurance runners are skilled at running long distances, right? Do they spend their time training on how to run fast or sprint? No, they spend countless hours perfecting their body's ability to go the distance.

Consider for a moment Lance Armstrong, the seven times Tour de France winner. Did you know that he didn't race other races? He specifically trained to win the tour year after year. His single goal and training regime was to train for and win the tour. That's why he won. He didn't let winning other races or even training for other races sidetrack him; he focused his skills and energies on the Tour de France completely and totally.

There's a common myth that says you need to strengthen your weaknesses. It's bogus. When you do that you end up with a bunch of fairly strong weaknesses at best. What you really need is to focus on your strengths and build those up so you can become AMAZING at your strengths – THAT is what will bring you success.

What are your Strengths Weaknesses Opportunities and Threats?

It is imperative to know what your strengths and opportunities are so that you may focus your time building them. They're the building blocks of your business and ultimately your successes. It is also important to understand your weaknesses and threats. Why? Because knowing and freely admitting your weaknesses and threats empowers you to let them go and be handled by someone whose strengths and opportunities they are.

Letting them go can be in the form of restructuring your business or business plan so your weaknesses aren't a significant part of your business. Or letting them go can mean outsourcing or hiring people whose strengths are your weaknesses.

For example, your strength may be writing. However, you're may be terrible at graphic design, formatting, and even editing and proofreading. It takes you a day to write a book and three weeks to make it look good. It would then make sense to spend that day writing and then hire someone else to make the book look good, right? You save yourself three weeks of frustration and lost income. While it may cost you $100 to have the book polished, you may make $5000 in that three weeks' time.

However, it is sometimes difficult both to recognize strengths and weaknesses and to admit them. This worksheet is designed to help you analyze both your strengths and weaknesses so you can make better business decisions going forward.

Strengths

Personal strengths form an innate part of who you are. Consider and answer the following in your notebook:

What skills and capabilities do you have?

In what areas do you excel?

What would other people consider to be your strengths?

What tasks do you find great pleasure in?

Weaknesses

Consider your personal weaknesses and how you think you are visualized by others. It is important to list any areas you feel may be holding you back. What are the gaps in your capabilities and skills?

What areas do you struggle in or find frustrating?

What would other people consider to be your weaknesses?

Opportunities

What opportunities are available to you to improve your strengths?

What external resources can help you to achieve success?

Who could support you to help you improve your strengths?

Threats

These are things that will get in the way of your success.

What obstacles are you facing that keep you from focusing on your strengths?

What external influences may hinder your success?

**EXTRA CREDIT: Go to www.kolbe.com and take the Kolbe A.

The Kolbe A measures a person's instinctive method of operation (MO), and identifies the ways he or she can be most productive and satisfied. Featured in Oprah magazine, it is a proven method of analyzing and getting at the core of who you are and how you work best. While it costs $50, it is totally worth the money and you only need to take it once to receive tremendous benefit.

More extra credit! Visit www.strengthsfinder.com and buy a copy of the book Strengths Finder 2.0 by Tom Rath. Inside the book you'll find a code to take an evaluation. Both the book and the evaluation are fantastic resources. You will learn more about yourself than you ever thought possible. That kind of information is powerful for anyone, but for an entrepreneur it is a time saving, life saving, money making resource, and it only costs $20.

Knowing your strengths is freeing and empowering at once. So often people have been conditioned to feel guilty about not performing well in areas where they are not strong. Playing to your strengths could be considered taking the easy way out because they're natural talents, not something you have to work for.

Regardless of your personal and spiritual beliefs, your strengths and talents are yours to make the most of. This is where you need to realize that you came here with certain strengths and talents for a reason, and if you're NOT strong in an area there's NOTHING wrong with that or with you. If it is something that is essential to your business, then find someone who IS strong in that area to compensate. Don't try to compensate yourself. It will end up as a mess, AND you'll be unhappy. The most logical and beneficial way to operate in life is to capitalize on your strengths and the strengths of others. When strengths are put together, powerful teams are built.

Sports are a perfect example of this. In American Football, the quarterback is good at throwing the ball - sometimes REALLY good at throwing the ball. They don't try to do anything else. They don't practice kicking, blocking, or catching the ball. The receivers are good at catching and running. The offensive line is good at protecting the quarterback and the defensive linebackers are great, hopefully, at getting through the offensive line and getting the opposing team's quarterback before he can throw the ball.

Together, when they capitalize on their strengths, they make it to the Super Bowl. When a player tries to be all things, the team suffers. One player doesn't make a team. One person doesn't make a company. Focus on your strengths, embrace your strengths, and find others who are strong where you are not to get the rest done.

Personal and Professional Development Tools

There are a number of tools available, like the personality tests in the extra credit assignment, for you to not only know who you are, but where you excel. There are also tools available to help you grow as a person and a professional. The three that stand out as truly productive and potentially powerful tools are outlined below.

Mastermind Groups

Mastermind groups are superb tools to stimulate the entrepreneurial spirit. They are groups of like-minded individuals who meet regularly, either in person, on the phone, or online. They challenge each other by helping to step out of the box to solve business problems, inspire each other to take steps into new arenas, and simply meet to help you hold yourself accountable for your business goals.

Mastermind groups are also excellent tools to learn more. The best groups are made up of people who are not in the same industries. This opens up the floor to learn more and to be exposed to new ideas and ways of doing business. It is important to make sure these are with supportive entrepreneurs who are at the same level as you are, or higher. You can mentor up-and-coming entrepreneurs at a separate time, but you need to be with people who are at your level and higher in order to grow.

Seminars, Online Courses, and Workshops

Continuing education is ESSENTIAL to growing your strengths and connecting with people who can fill in for other areas. In fact, it is common for top entrepreneurs to plan continuing education into their goals, business plan, and lifestyle. While this may seem like a time-consuming and non-profit generating exercise, the opposite is actually very true.

Seminars, workshops, courses, and guides like this one will actually stimulate ideas that will generate profits. The time spent in these endeavors is worth it. You'll walk out a wiser, better-rounded, and invigorated person. Being stimulated by new ideas, concepts, and ways of doing business is imperative to continued growth and success.

Learning Style Inventory

Knowing your strengths and weaknesses is important in order to know how best to plan your time. Knowing how you learn, and how to interact with people that learn differently, will make your business interactions more productive, pleasant, and profitable too. We all have preferred ways of receiving information. You may be familiar with the visual, auditory, and kinesthetic modes of processing information and interacting.

Visual learners learn by seeing and reading, auditory learners learn by listening and speaking, and kinesthetic learners learn by touching and doing. It is possible to have a mixed or even a balanced blend of two or three of these styles. We may function in any of the styles as circumstances change. There is no right vs. wrong or better vs. undesirable style or mix of styles.

What matters is that we understand both how we communicate and how others communicate so we can work together effectively and without frustrations. To explore the learning modalities and how best to communicate with people who are dominant in each one, check out the Crystal Clear Communication Guide, Lesson 2.

> *"Change is the law of life. And those who look only to the past or the present are certain to miss the future."*
> *– John F. Kennedy*

Planning for the Future: Continuous Development and Assessment

Just as it is important to pull out the business plan on a regular basis and evaluate where you are, where you want to improve, and what needs to be changed or re-evaluated, it is also important to do that for yourself. Regular assessment of your strengths, skills, and how to handle your weaknesses and grow your strengths is important. Just like the business world changes, so do you. You are in a constant state of evolution.

Why it is Important to Plan for the Future

Someone once said that there is one true fact in life: things will change. That includes you. When you spend time evaluating how you've changed and where you want to go, you can plan for the future. You can seek guides, people, and situations to help you continue to grow. Consider the life of a professional business coach. One of their strengths is probably going to be people skills, but also knowledge of the tools available to enable business people to be productive, efficient, and so on. It is in that coach's best interest to continue to develop their knowledge and their people skills.

What You Have to Gain

The bottom line for most people thinking in a business mindset is profits. Yes, as you continue to develop, reassess your strengths, and plan for the future, you have profits to gain. You're going to continue to improve and strengthen, and that in return will drive profits, assuming you're also managing your business and your weaknesses. However, life is more than profits and business, right?

Consider what happens to you as a person if you plan to continually improve your strengths. What do you have to gain? Satisfaction with your job. Pride in your accomplishments. Mental stimulation and self-awareness. Those are three pretty good benefits, right? All you have to do is sit back and do a self-evaluation from time to time, pull out your personal "plan" and look at it with an eye to the future. How can you continue to stay on top of your game and receive the benefits of doing so?

How Much Time Do You Spend on Yourself?

T. Harv Eker recommends that you spend 10% of your resources (time & income) on your education. YOU are your greatest asset as well as your business' biggest asset, especially in the early stages. You HAVE to spend your time and resources educating yourself and building your strengths.

> *"A formal education will make you a living, but self-education will make you a fortune."*
> *- Jim Rohn*

Let's look at how are you going to take care of your weaknesses. Notice we said "take care of", not "improve upon" or "strengthen".

It is important to recognize that you, along with everyone else, are born with intrinsic strengths. Focus on those and find a way to take care of the weaknesses. It may mean hiring an expert. It may mean changing your strategy to focus on your strengths. Brainstorm here. Consider the questions and prompts below and record answers, thoughts, and ideas in your notebook.

How are you going to take care of your weaknesses?

Brainstorm possibilities and outline an action plan.

> *"Twenty years from now you will be more disappointed by the things that you didn't do than by the ones you did do. So throw off the bowlines. Sail away from the safe harbor. Catch the trade winds in your sails. Explore. Dream. Discover."*
> *- Mark Twain*

Lesson 3: Having a Life Outside of the Business

Entrepreneurs are generally serial workaholics. Therefore it is important to keep in mind why we started a business to begin with. There are many clichés we could toss in here. Life is for the living, you only live once…and so on. The point is that there is more to life than being an entrepreneur. You are a multifaceted person with plenty to offer, both personally and professionally.

When the professional side of life takes over and squeezes out the personal side, life tips out of balance. The effect? Burnout, boredom, stress, illness, and lack of a smile on your face (which, believe it or not will affect your profits). Who wants to do business with someone that isn't enjoying life or what they do?

While every day may not be a smile day, when life is in balance, it is much easier to smile, have fun, and enjoy life.

So how do you get, and keep, life in balance?

Let's begin by taking a look at where your life is right now.

Evaluating Your Priorities

Balance is a continuous tightrope to walk. However, once you know where your priorities lie, it is much easier to devote time, plan ahead, and achieve balance. For many, this exercise may be an eye-opener. Answer the questions honestly because we're going to use this information as a launching point to bring your life into balance.

Step 1. In your notebook, write down the ten most important things in your life (i.e. children, spouse, business, pet.)

Step 2. Rank them. Go back and recreate the list, putting your most important priority on line one and the least important priority on line ten.

Step 3. Refer to the list you just made and document how much of your week or month you spend on each of the 10 items. For example 10% on spouse, 20% on children...Not how much time you WANT to spend on these priorities, but how much time you ACTUALLY spend.

Now, look at your responses, and ask yourself the following:

How much time are you spending on what is truly important to you?

Is it as much time as you thought?

Is it as much time as you want it to be?

For many of us, the answer to the last question is probably not. Most of us work more than we want to and don't spend enough time with our families or doing the things we really enjoy. Even if you enjoy your work (and we hope that you do), it is still important to have a life that is separate, fulfilling, and enjoyable.

So what are you going to do about it?

Go back and look at your list and write down how much time you WANT to spend on those priorities.

Great, now let's take a look at what you can do to make this a reality!

Ric Thompson

> *"Life must be lived and curiosity kept alive. One must never, for whatever reason, turn his back on life."*
> — Eleanor Roosevelt

Is Your Life in Balance?

Consider this example: George, a software developer, started a business five years ago. George is an educated man with a Harvard business degree and brains to boot. He knows how to make money, and he's good at it. Not only is he good at developing software, primarily medium to large business storage technologies, he's also good at selling his products. He believes in them and the enthusiasm for his work comes through when he speaks. George also has a family. A beautiful wife who is a published author, and two elementary-school-aged children.

When George started his business, his enthusiasm was contagious. Friends, family, and associates were supportive and life was good. As you know, being an entrepreneur is time-consuming. For George it was incredibly time-consuming. Not only did he spend about 40 hours a week developing products, he also spent about 40 hours a week selling them. Much of that time was on the road. Spending 80 hours a week building a business doesn't leave much time for the family. It doesn't leave much time for anything.

Now George's family wasn't the kind to put their heads in the sand. They stood up and told George things had to change. His life was out of balance, they were feeling his absence, and people were beginning to become unhappy. At this point, George had built his business to a level where he could easily have hired people to handle the majority of the selling or the product development, without losing customers or quality, but he didn't. He persisted with the lifestyle because he didn't know how to get out of it.

Guess what happened to George?

His wife has a new life without him. His children now live in another state.

You'd think those changes would be enough to motivate George to adapt and begin to seek balance. However, the absence of his family only served to immerse him more into his business. Unfortunately, what often happens in such a case happened to George. He became so one-dimensional that his business began to suffer. It didn't happen quickly, but one by one, customers began to fall away. Why? George, while still single-minded about the success of his company, began to lose enthusiasm for his business, and, in fact, his life. This lack of enthusiasm is contagious. People sense it, and when you're not engaged in life and in your business they know it. They fall away.

George, once sitting on top of what could have been a perfect life, now works in a standard white-collar job as a programmer. His business is gone, his beautiful family is gone. The man who almost had it all, lost it all because he didn't realize how important a balanced life really is.

Why did this happen to George? What does this story have to teach?

Well, the biggest thing that happened to George is the loss of his family. Additionally, his business is gone. Sad really, when the steps to live a balanced life are really pretty straightforward. (We'll get into them in just a bit, I promise!)

Setting George's sad story aside for a moment – a lack of balance can result in becoming completely disenchanted with being an entrepreneur. What would have happened if Henry

Ford had neglected the other aspects of his life? He didn't. He had many children and many other passions, including the fact that he built and drove race cars. He financed a pacifist expedition to Europe during WWI. He was an unsuccessful candidate for the United States Senate in 1918. He owned a controversial newspaper, The Dearborn Independent, which published anti-Jewish articles which offended many and tarnished his image. Henry Ford established schools in several areas of the country, which provided educational experiences based on traditional one-room school techniques, modern teaching methods, and "learning through doing". He also established an indoor/outdoor museum – The Henry Ford – to preserve historical items that illustrated the American experience and American ingenuity. Whatever you think of the man, his business, or his politics, Henry Ford had many passions and interests outside of his passion to bring the automobile to the mass market, and THAT is a big part of what made him successful.

So, what's the point? If your business is your entire life, life will eventually become pretty dull and meaningless.

> *"Work, love, and play are the great balance wheels of man's being."*
> *- Orison Swett Marden*

Without Balance We Neglect the Things that are Really Important to Us

It isn't okay to neglect the things that are important to you. You will suffer the consequences.

For example, if working out every morning is important to you, and you change your routine and decide to spend mornings researching your website statistics and going over profit reports, you're denying yourself something that is deeply important to you. You may not feel the effects right away, but after a month or two of skipping workouts, you will begin to feel the effects both physically and mentally.

If spending Friday nights with your family having dinner and a family game night has been important to you in the past, make sure it stays important to you in the present and in the future. Not just because it is important to your family, but because it is important to you. Business can wait. Tasks can be delegated and profits can wait. Your life is important too.

The Benefits of Living a Balanced Life

You've seen the downside of living out of balance. Now consider this story:

Charlie always dreamed of making a career in the fitness industry. About two years ago, she took the leap and became a certified personal instructor. Now, certification alone isn't enough to bring customers to your door. Being a profitable personal instructor means marketing, a lot of marketing, and networking. Both of these things are time-consuming. Additionally, she had to continue to stay in shape and compete to keep her credibility as a personal instructor.

On top of these requirements, Charlie learned that there is a constant influx of new information. Not just diet and sports nutrition information, which clients invariably want to know about, but also medical and physical information. Science is continuously moving forward, as are fitness trends. Not only did Charlie need to know about Tae Bo, she also needed to know about spinning and every other new fitness trend. Clients invariably ask about what's new, and she wanted to stay on top of her game and know what she was talking about. For the first six months Charlie was overwhelmed by the demands on her time. In addition she was a newlywed and had a new baby.

It actually got to the point where Charlie began to rethink being a business owner. Before losing her sanity, Charlie decided to do a couple of things. She knew her profits came from her one-on-one consultation with her clients. It was also what she enjoyed the most. She focused her time on these tasks and hired a web designer. She also set aside one day a month to attend marketing or networking functions and one day a month to upgrade her knowledge. She scheduled her time so that she could work out in the early mornings.

Charlie decided to not see clients on the weekends and set aside that time specifically for her husband and her new baby. Additionally, she decided that three nights a week she'd see clients, but Monday and Friday were for her. Also, she ended her day at 3:00 so she could take her baby to "Mommy and Me" classes.

In short, Charlie found balance. The ability to set boundaries between her professional and personal life, and to keep those boundaries, helped her stay in the moment, which meant truly engaged sessions with her clients and truly engaged time with her family. She wasn't torn between priorities because she'd made time for them.

One year after opening her business, Charlie hired an assistant trainer who she worked into her clients' schedules. The assistant now rotates sessions, giving Charlie even more time to both work with new clients and build her business. Life is good.

As you can see from Charlie's story, when balance is achieved (and it isn't always easy), then both your personal life and your professional life can thrive and prosper. One doesn't have to suffer at the expense of the other. The key is to make time for both.

A balanced life means:

Happiness

When a life is in balance, everything works better. We're not saying that everything runs smoothly, but the bumps in the road are more easily managed.

A Sense of Peace and Calm

Stress is reduced. When you take time to relax, laugh, do the things you love to do, and let go of business for a while, it is easier to go back to the business of doing business.

Better Run Business

Imagine not taking a vacation for a year. Imagine working an 80 hour week. You barely have time to eat and sleep, and all your attention is devoted to business. What happens? Stress. Unhappiness. Decisions based on panic mode or stress. A lack of perspective. These are all bad for business.

However, when you take time away, you have a renewed perspective, you reduce or eliminate stress, and your happiness is increased. All of these factors make it easier for you to make good decisions for you and your business. The result? A continued life in balance and a better business. It's a circle of success and balance.

Is Your Life in Balance?

Answer true or false to each statement below in your notebook.

1. I find myself spending more and more time on work-related projects.

2. I often feel I don't have any time for myself, my family, or my friends.

3. No matter what I do, it often seems that every minute of every day is always scheduled for something.

4. Sometimes I feel as though I've lost sight of who I am and why I chose to go into business.

5. I can't remember when I was last able to find the time to take a day off to do something fun.

6. I feel stressed out most of the time.

7. It sometimes feels as though I never even have a chance to catch my breath before I have to move on to the next project/crisis.

8. I wish I had more time for some outside interests and hobbies.

9. I've missed many of my family's important events because of work-related time pressures and responsibilities.

10. I almost always bring work home with me.

If you have three or more True statements, your life is out of balance.

Tools to Bring Balance to Your Life

There is a ton of ways to balance your life. Balance is personal and it is relative to the person. What is balance for you may not be balance for someone else. Only you know if your life is in or out of balance. So while it is important to assess your life regularly and find your own tightrope to balance on, there are tools to help you structure your life to have more balance. We're not talking about tangible tools. You can't find balance with a screwdriver or a pocket planner. These tools are more like strategies for a balanced life and they work for everyone.

The absolute first thing anyone and everyone must do is set priorities for their life. At the beginning of this guide, you took an evaluation and gave yourself a score. When your score is a perfect 10, you're living a balanced life. Make a list of what is important to you and how important it is.

Are you prioritizing the right things?

Are you doing what is important to you?

This may seem small, but if you used to work out every day and personal health and fitness is important to you, but you've let it slide since becoming an entrepreneur, you're probably feeling the effects, right? Set time aside to get back into a fitness routine. It doesn't have to be an hour every day, though it can be. Something as simple as 30 minutes every other day may help you feel like you're fitting the right things into your life and finding balance.

The second strategy for balance is scheduling time to do nothing. Seriously. If you don't do this, life will do it for you in the form of a virus or injury – so do it for yourself and avoid the discomfort. Schedule days off. Schedule weeks off. Schedule months off if you can. Simply allow yourself to sit back and rest.

Mark Victor Hansen, the *Chicken Soup for the Soul* guy, takes one week of vacation per month to keep in balance. The other three weeks he works extremely hard. What is that phrase, work hard, play hard?

What is fun for you? Spending time reading? Spending time with friends? Going to the movies? Snowboarding or hitting the local amusement park and jumping on the most intense roller coaster? Fun has its role in life. Laughter, friends, entertainment are all just as important as business and profit – actually, they are more important.

> *"Live and work but do not forget to play,*
> *to have fun in life and really enjoy it."*
> *- Eileen Caddy*

Without fun in our lives, we lose our smile. Fun gives us something to look forward to. Something to hang on to when things are tough.

Enjoy what you're doing, and focus on it when you're doing it. If you're thinking about that business call you have to make while your child is sharing a story about what happened at school, you're missing the joy in the story. Living in the moment doesn't have to be at the exclusion of the future; you can be aware of that business call and still give your child 100% attention. Likewise if you're talking to a client, you don't want to be thinking about what movie you're going to see this weekend. Give each moment your full attention and then move on to whatever is next on your schedule, plan, or agenda.

Allow yourself to live in the moment and the future at the same time (most entrepreneurs can be overly focused on the future and neglect the present). Too many people can be so focused on "living in the moment," that they neglect to intend and plan for the future. Look at the hit film "The Secret." If you're intending and creating the future, you're not living in the moment, but if you're strictly living in the moment, then you can't intend and create your future. As with everything, there's a balance, so don't get sucked in by pithy pop-culture quips or even spiritual/religious dogma. Entrepreneurs, above all things, think for themselves.

> *"Believe nothing, no matter where you read it or who has said it, not even if I have said it, unless it agrees with your own reason and your own common sense."*
> *-Buddha*

What anyone chooses to do or believe or act on, whether in business or in life, is up to them as long as they have analyzed it first and CONSCIOUSLY chosen it. Entrepreneurs must, on a regular basis, question conventional wisdom, look at their own limiting and empowering beliefs, and see how those beliefs do or don't serve them. An entrepreneur is in the business of creating their own life and their own world and must be responsible for all beliefs and how they affect the world of their business.

Another must for a successful entrepreneur and a balanced life is to ask for help. Seriously. Your job isn't to do everything. You're not required to be a lawyer, accountant, sales person, copywriter, customer service representative, public relations expert, and marketer and so on. Your job is to focus on your strengths and get help! We address this in detail in Section Four of the Business Management Guide.

Learn to say no. This isn't advice. This is a necessity. Your job as an entrepreneur isn't to make everyone happy. A boss I once told me this, "Tell the customer yes and then figure out how to make it happen." As a young person in the business world I thought, okay. Once I owned my own business, I quickly realized that was total crap. Sometimes, whether it is the customer you're talking to, or a business associate or a potential partner, you have to say no. Being an entrepreneur isn't about pleasing folks, it's about making your business the best it can be. If you have trouble saying no, take an assertiveness class and re-read the section on Negotiation in the Business Strategy Guide. You can also check out my Confidence Guide for help. If there isn't a benefit for you and your business, then it isn't worth your time. Trust me, people will say no to you. It isn't personal, it's practical.

Let go of perfection. Perfection doesn't exist. Even in the bluest of skies there are clouds, airplanes, bugs, and birds. Perfection is an excuse to procrastinate. To avoid committing. It takes too much time and it drains your productivity. Nothing is perfect. Do your best, and let it go. No one expects perfection, they do expect you to do your best.

Take care of yourself. A balanced life isn't complete without some thought toward your health. This isn't a guide on how to eat right and take care of your body, but it is an important part of living a balanced and happy life. If you're too sick to work then you're too sick to play. We all get sick from time to time. It's usually a sign from our bodies that something is out of balance. Take care of it, and it'll stay in balance.

How are You Going to Add More Fun to Your Life?

When was the last time you had fun? Hopefully it was yesterday! Whether it was yesterday or last month, think back to the last time you had real fun. Close your eyes, and remember how you felt. How did you feel the next day going back to work? How did you feel the day before you had fun?

What's the point? Fun brings balance into your life. It makes the difficult days easier to get through, it gives you something to look forward to, and it changes your perspective on life. Imagine working 24/7 and never making time to enjoy life. Work suffers, health suffers, life suffers. However, even the simplest things, like going to the movies or playing board games with friends and family, can be tremendously fun and rewarding.

Fun doesn't have to be a tropical vacation, though it can be! Fun can be reading a great book, going for a walk in the woods, playing with your dog or meeting friends for dinner downtown. Fun is relative to the individual and it is important!

As you make your way through this exercise, keep in mind what is fun for you. There are no expectations. This exercise is simply designed to get you thinking about what you want from your life and how you're going to get it!

How are you going to balance your life?

List ten fun things you'd like to do or learn in the next twelve months. (For example, go skydiving, learn to ballroom dance, join a club)

Prioritize them. What's number one? Now plan how you're going to accomplish it.

EXTRA CREDIT: If you're a Type A overachiever and workaholic, this is a requirement – not just extra credit. Take a few hours and listen to the audio book version of Tim Ferris' 4-Hour Workweek. You can listen in the car or while you're working out if you must, but be sure to listen. It will change the way you view your work and quite possibly your life.

Life is for living. Business is important, but it is only a part of your complete life. When you're living your life with a purpose and have your priorities straight, you're less stressed, and your business will run more smoothly.

In this guide, we've talked about the importance of knowing your strengths and your weaknesses. We've given you the tools to assess them, including some extra credit tools to really increase your awareness, power, and effectiveness as an entrepreneur. We've given you the tools to focus on your strengths and manage your time in the most productive and effective manner possible.

We've emphasized the importance of building on your strengths and "handling" your weaknesses. We've talked about the importance of personal and professional growth through interaction with others, by taking guides, seminars, and workshops, and by continuously evaluating how you can improve and become a better person and professional.

We've ended this guide with a discussion about the importance of a balanced life. This is an area not to be glossed over because it can make or break you as a person and as a professional.

Harry Truman said, "I studied the lives of great men and famous women, and I found that the men and women who got to the top were those who did the jobs they had in hand, with everything they had of energy and enthusiasm and hard work."

The key to being able to maintain enthusiasm and work hard is to balance your life, find joy, take time off, and most importantly remember your priorities.

Remember what you have to offer to this world. Entrepreneurs are life-altering forces. We need you. You're the butterfly flapping its wings and changing the guide of future. Take this responsibility, this magnificent privilege, and use it to the best of your ability.

Inspired Action

Here's where we pull it all together and put it into action.

Go back through your notes and the responses to the exercises and list all of your targets, goals, and action steps:

- What steps are you going to take to better manage your time? What tools will you use?

- We all have strengths and weaknesses. How are you going to grow? What steps will you take to develop your skills?

- How can you better keep your life in balance?

List one item per line, and after you have them all listed, rank each one in order of priority. Rank the one that will make the biggest impact in your business and your life RIGHT NOW as number 1, the second as number 2, and so on down the list.

Take the top three and create a SMART Plan for each one. Work those plans until you hit the target, then come back, and create a SMART Plan for the next three. Remember, SMART plans must include:

S – pecific

M – easurable

A – ttainable

R – ealistic

T – ime Trackable

What's Your Entrepreneurial Score NOW?

It's time to retake the evaluation you took at the beginning of the guide.

It is important to see how much progress you've made since the beginning of this guide. You now have incredible tools to not only balance your time, but also to prioritize it for maximum profit and enjoyment. These are the keys to being a successful entrepreneur, to being the kind of entrepreneur that can change the world. It all begins right here, with you. Take this evaluation again and see how much you've changed, grown, and learned in such a short amount of time.

On a scale of 1-10 (10 being the highest), rank where you currently stand in life and in business. Once you've completed this guide, you'll be taking this evaluation again to see where you've improved.

I know the exact dollar value of my time.

1   2   3   4   5   6   7   8   9   10

I know what my strengths are and have systems in place to help my focus on them.

1   2   3   4   5   6   7   8   9   10

I know what my weaknesses are and have plans for how to get other people to handle them for me.

1   2   3   4   5   6   7   8   9   10

I have systems in place to effectively and efficiently manage my time

1   2   3   4   5   6   7   8   9   10

I know what my time priorities are and have a plan for how to make sure my business doesn't take over my entire life

1   2   3   4   5   6   7   8   9   10

I am confident that I can drive my business, not have my business drive me.

1   2   3   4   5   6   7   8   9   10

SCORING

Add up all the numbers you circled.   _____

Divide the total number by 6

Record your NEW "Entrepreneurial Score" here

_____

Did you see an improvement in your score? Why do you think you did or did not?

Come back in a month, six months, or even a year, and retake the assessment to see how your knowledge and use of your business strategy has changed your business outcomes.

Conclusion

Congratulations on your decision to join the world of the entrepreneur!

Taking the critical steps outlined in this guide will help you to ensure that your business is as strong and profitable as possible! Being an entrepreneur isn't easy, but by taking these steps and learning to manage your time effectively, you're ensuring a stronger business and a better life for you and your family.

> **"Working for someone else is nothing like being an entrepreneur and the boss of your own business. To become an entrepreneur requires a different plan or map. You'll be taking a different road, to a different destination."**
> - *Noel Peebles, Author of Sell Your Business the Easy Way*

When you have all of these factors accounted for, then and only then can you plan to be in that winning percentage of businesses that are still around and thriving five years from now.

This book provided you with valuable insights into the world of the entrepreneur. You learned:

- What it means to be an entrepreneur
- Why time management is crucial for entrepreneurs
- How to determine the value of your time
- How to more effectively manage your time
- How to choose time management tools that work for you
- Why you need to know yourself to be successful

- How important it is to set aside time for personal development
- Why you need to have a life outside of your business
- How to evaluate and analyze your priorities
- Why living a balanced life matters
- How to get more fun in your life
- How to create a SMART plan to turn your innovation inspiration into action

Now it's time to take what you have learned and make a difference in your business. Remember, being an entrepreneur means you are the boss!

Ric Thompson

Check out Ric's other books!!

http://www.amazon.com/dp/B00I3Q2QPK

http://www.amazon.com/dp/B00LIGKRCG

Being an Entrepreneur

http://www.amazon.com/dp/B00H4HHY56

http://www.amazon.com/dp/B00L9K6928

www.ingramcontent.com/pod-product-compliance
Lightning Source LLC
Chambersburg PA
CBHW071802170526
45167CB00003B/1142